HISTORY OPENS WINDOWS

The
MAYA

JANE SHUTER

Heinemann Library
Chicago, Illinois

Designed by Roslyn Broder
Printed in Hong Kong

06 05 04 03 02
10 9 8 7 6 5 4 3 2 1

Library of Congress Cataloging-in-Publication Data
Shuter, Jane.
    The Maya / Jane Shuter.
        p. cm. – (History opens windows)
Includes bibliographical references and index.
Summary: Presents an overview of the Mayan culture, discussing
their government, religion, domestic life, recreation, occupations,
entertainment, food, shelter, and clothing.
    ISBN 1-58810-591-1 (lib. bdg.)   ISBN 1-4034-0026-1 (pbk. bdg.)
    1. Mayas – History – Juvenile literature. 2. Mayas – Social life and
    customs – Juvenile literature. [1. Mayas. 2. Indians of Central
    America.] I. Title. II. Series.
F1435 .S546 2002
972.81'01—dc21

                                       2001004028

Acknowledgments
The author and publishers are grateful to the following for permission to reproduce copyright material:
p. 6 Kimbell Art Museum/Corbis; pp. 7, 18, 21, 23, 25 © Justin Kerr; p. 8 Werner Forman/Art
Resource; p. 10 Michael Freeman/Corbis; p. 11 Charles and Josette Lenars/Corbis; pp. 12, 13 Gianni
Dagli Orti/Corbis; pp. 14, 20, 28 D. Donne Bryant/Art Resource; p. 16 Eric Lessing/Art Resource;
pp. 19, 30 SEF/Art Resource; p. 22 Michel Zabe/Art Resource; p. 24 Dr. Kurt Stavenhagen Collection,
Mexico City/Werner Forman/Art Resource; p. 26 Owen Franken/Corbis; p. 29 Scala/Art Resource

Illustrations: p. 4 Eileen Mueller Neill; pp. 9, 15, 17, 27 Juvenal "Marty" Martinez
Cover photograph courtesy of Eric Lessing/Art Resource

Every effort has been made to contact copyright holders of any material reproduced in this book.
Any omissions will be rectified in subsequent printings if notice is given to the publisher.

Some words are shown in bold, **like this.** You can find out what they mean by
looking in the glossary.

A note about dates: in this book, dates are followed by the letters B.C.E. (Before the
Common Era) or C.E. (Common Era). This instead of using the older abbreviations B.C.
and A.D. The date numbers are the same in both systems.

Contents

Introduction 4

How Were the Maya Ruled? 6

City-States 8

Building a City 10

Religion 12

Ballcourts 14

Temples and Burials 16

War 18

Food and Farming 20

Trade and Work 22

Families and Clothing 24

Homes 26

Writing and Calendars 28

End of Empire 30

Glossary 31

More Books to Read 31

Pronunciation Guide 32

Index 32

Introduction

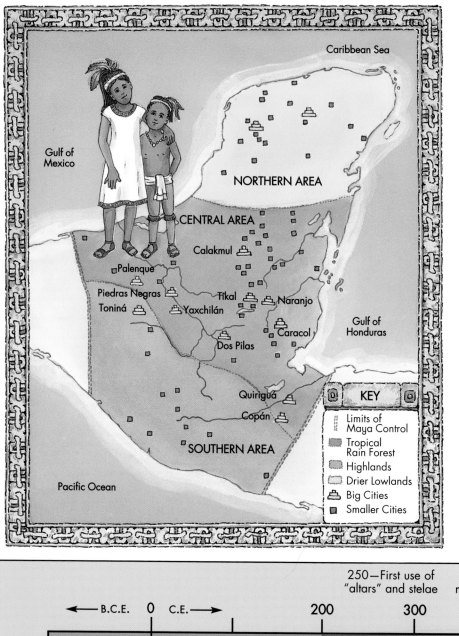

Caribbean Sea

Gulf of Mexico

NORTHERN AREA

CENTRAL AREA

Calakmul

Palenque

Piedras Negras

Tikal

Naranjo

Toniná   Yaxchilán

Gulf of Honduras

Caracol

Dos Pilas

Quiriguá

Copán

SOUTHERN AREA

Pacific Ocean

KEY

Limits of Maya Control
Tropical Rain Forest
Highlands
Drier Lowlands
Big Cities
Smaller Cities

This map shows lands the Maya lived in and ruled.

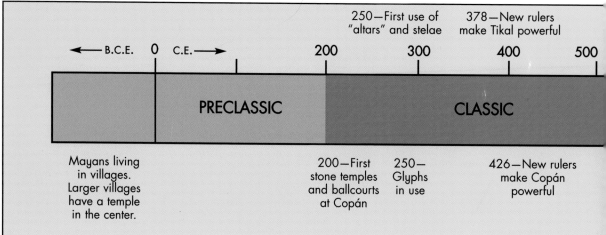

250—First use of "altars" and stelae

378—New rulers make Tikal powerful

← B.C.E.   0   C.E. →   200   300   400   500

PRECLASSIC   **CLASSIC**

Mayans living in villages. Larger villages have a temple in the center.

200—First stone temples and ballcourts at Copán

250—Glyphs in use

426—New rulers make Copán powerful

4

The Maya were a group of people who became powerful in Central America from about 250 C.E. to 900 C.E. Today, the land they controlled covers Guatemala, Belize, and parts of Mexico.

The land and climate of the area settled by the Maya made farming and building difficult. There were mountains in the south and rain forests in the center. Despite this, the Maya farmed the land and built cities with huge stone palaces and **temples.**

We see the Maya as a single group, even though many different kings ruled the **city-states.** The Maya shared a religion, organized themselves in the same way, and used the same written language. They also used the same calendar system and a similar building style.

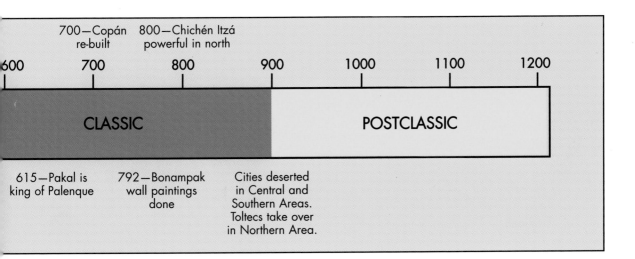

5

How Were the Maya Ruled?

The Maya did not have a single ruler. Each city and the lands around it were ruled by a different *ajaw* (pronounced ah-HAW). An *ajaw* spoke to the gods for his people. He took part in many **ceremonies** wearing masks to show different gods.

Each *ajaw* was seen as chosen by the gods. Sometimes sons ruled after their fathers, so historians think the Maya believed the gods chose a family to rule, not just one person.

This clay statue shows a Mayan ajaw, *dressed for a religious ceremony.*

An *ajaw* ruled with the help of **nobles,** priests, and officials. He lived with his family and servants in a palace in the city. Women rarely ruled, although some queens ruled for their young sons until they grew up.

Almost all ordinary people lived in villages and farmed the land. They only went to the cities for religious ceremonies and other **festivals.**

Most Mayan rulers were men. There were only a few women rulers. But the wives of the ajaws were important and took part in religious ceremonies. Here, the wife of Bird Jaguar is shown having a vision of a serpent ancestor.

City-States

Historians call a Maya city and the land it controlled a **city-state.** Some city-states were more powerful than others. Also, different city-states were powerful at different times. They fought each other and traded with each other. A small city-state often needed a powerful city-state to protect it from its enemies. Its *ajaw* was king of his city, but he had to obey the *ajaw* of his protecting city.

This stone carving shows a captured **noble** kneeling in front of the ajaw "Bird Jaguar," whose army has beaten him. The prisoner is biting his fingers as a sign that he is giving in.

The *ajaw,* his family, and a large group of nobles, priests, and officials lived in the city. The only ordinary people we know about who lived in the cities were servants. Most ordinary people lived in nearby villages. The villagers grew and made almost everything they needed. They had to grow enough food to feed the people in the cities too. This was part of their duty to the *ajaw.*

This modern artist's recreation shows part of the city of Copán, looking from the central square to the temple area. All the buildings in this area are temples except for the ballcourt.

Ballcourt

9

Building a City

All buildings in the cities were made from local stone. Most Maya cities had sources of limestone nearby. In the city of Copán, the builders used a **volcanic** stone. It was soft when it was dug out, but it hardened over time.

Every city had a Great **Plaza,** where the most important **temples** and the royal palace were built. The rest of the city spread out from the plaza. Big cities had several smaller plazas with temples and other public buildings in them.

Temples led to the sky, the home of the gods, so they were designed to look as tall as possible.

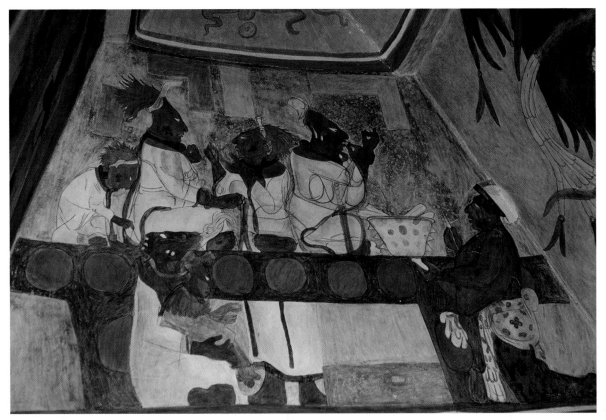

In this decorated room at Bonampak, you can see the shape of the corbeled roof. It has been covered with slabs to make a smooth line.

Temples and palaces had the same steep shape as the **thatched** roofs of ordinary homes. To get this shape, the builders made a series of steps. Each layer of stones was smaller than the layer below. This is called corbeling. The steps were then filled in or covered over, making a smooth, sloping surface.

Most palaces and temples were probably decorated on the inside. The brightly-colored pictures of people, animals, and gods each told a story.

Religion

"Altar stones" like this one were placed in front of many temples. We think that the Maya put offerings to the gods on them. **Ajaws** *may have stood on them during religious* **ceremonies.**

The Maya believed in many gods and goddesses. They controlled every part of life, from how the crops grew, to a person's health, to which **city-state** won a war. The Maya kept the gods happy by praying and performing dances, music, and plays. They also gave gifts to the gods, including food and often blood.

The Maya religion taught that without gifts of blood, the gods would stop the sun, the rain, and everything else. So a king or priest would give some of his blood in a bowl. But sometimes the gods wanted a whole life—an animal or a human, most often prisoners captured in wars.

The Maya also believed that the **spirits** of dead relatives could affect their daily lives. These spirits needed gifts, too. They could help you if you were in trouble, but if you did not keep them happy they could cause trouble. Most ordinary people had a **shrine** in their homes. This was a special place where they could pray to their dead relatives.

This pottery oil burner was used in religious ceremonies. It shows an old god sitting on a stool and was found buried with a **noble** *in Tikal.*

13

Ballcourts

The Maya played a ball game in villages and cities with two teams and a hard rubber ball on a long, thin court. In the villages, the courts were just a straight, flat piece of land. In the cities the ball game became linked to Maya religious beliefs, and they built stone ballcourts near the **temples.** At important **festivals,** Maya kings played the ball game to defeat death, darkness, and **famine.** They were copying an old story in which the Lords of the Underworld were beaten at a ball game.

The ballcourt at Copán was built right next to a temple. This shows how the game was sometimes linked to religious festivals.

The rules of the ball game are not clear. They may even have been different in different places and at different times.

There were two teams. The number of players on a team was not always the same, but there were probably no more than five.

The ball was not allowed to touch the ground.

The ball was kept moving by bouncing it off the side of the ballcourt.

The object of the game was to get to ball into the open end of the other team's end of the court.

Temples and Burials

Temples were the homes of the gods. They were the tallest buildings in a Maya city, and the Maya called them "mountains." The shrine at the top, the house of the god, was very small and looked like an ordinary Maya house. But because it was a home for a god it was built from stone, which ordinary houses were not. It was also beautifully decorated, inside and out, with carvings and paintings.

This burial mask was made from jade in about 527 C.E. Burial masks were put over the faces of ajaws and nobles as part of the burial ceremony.

Many Maya temples are more than they seem. There are probably several other layers under the temple that you can see. Maya kings often rebuilt temples to show how important they thought the gods were. Temples also often hide a king's tomb. Kings were buried under tombs with the things they would need after death, like clothes and food. Ordinary people were buried under their homes.

The tomb of Pakal, king of Palenque, lies deep under the Temple of the Inscriptions in Palenque.

War

An *ajaw* had to prove that he was a good fighter and war leader. This is because Maya **city-states** often fought each other. They did not have a full-time army, but the **nobles** were trained as fighters. The Maya tried to capture their enemies instead of killing them. Enemy kings were often forced to play the ball game at religious **festivals.** The *ajaw* would make sure that the captured king lost.

Many Maya carvings show an ajaw *who has won a war having his defeated enemies brought to him. It showed his strength and importance. This carving shows captives being brought to Shield Jaguar in 783.*

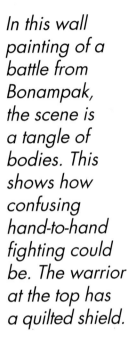

In this wall painting of a battle from Bonampak, the scene is a tangle of bodies. This shows how confusing hand-to-hand fighting could be. The warrior at the top has a quilted shield.

The Maya went to war to the sound of trumpets and drums. They fought hand-to-hand, not in organized groups. Their weapons were clubs and stone-tipped spears. They also used daggers with stone blades. For defense, warriors carried small handheld shields and armor made from many layers of **quilted** cotton cloth.

A warrior could surrender during a battle if he knelt down and held another warrior's leg. Being captured was not always a bad thing for a noble warrior. Some were killed, but others settled down in their new city-states and began a new life.

Food and Farming

The Maya farmed the land around their villages, using digging sticks to turn over the soil. They tried to plant two crops a year.

In some areas, farmers grew food on **terraces** to keep the soil from washing away in heavy rain or floods. In other places they built ponds to trap water for **irrigating** the fields. But they mostly used the slash-and-burn method. This involves cutting down the trees and plants in a field, then burning them. Then they planted crops in the ash mixed with soil and let the rain water them.

It was hard to clear the lowland jungle and make the land suitable for farming.

Maya farmers grew corn, beans, and squash in the fields. They also grew avocados, cocoa beans, and fruit trees. There were gardens in the villages where people grew tomatoes, chilis, and peppers. The Maya hunted animals, such as rabbits and deer, for meat. They also fished in rivers or in the sea, if they lived near the coast.

The Maya cooked their food over an open fire. They either roasted it or stewed it in a pot in the flames. Ordinary people mainly ate corn porridge, flat bread made with corn flour, and vegetables.

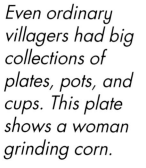

Even ordinary villagers had big collections of plates, pots, and cups. This plate shows a woman grinding corn.

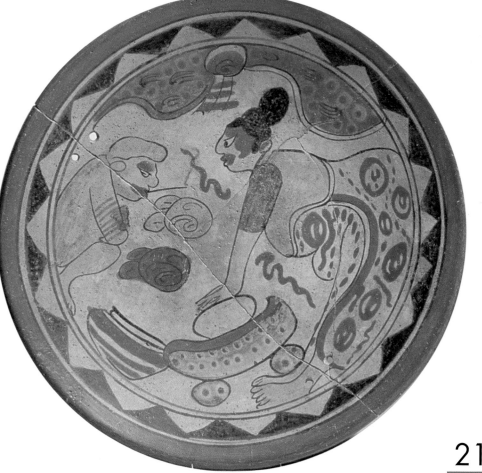

21

Trade and Work

Maya villages grew or made most of the things they needed. They did not trade very much. Traders mostly brought back goods for people in the cities.

Skilled craft workers lived in many cities, making things for the kings, **nobles,** and priests. Traders brought back pottery and jewelry as well as raw materials for craft workers to use, such as feathers, shells, and precious stones.

This jade jar was buried with one of the royal family in Tikal. Only very important people could afford such beautiful things. Green jade was the most valuable kind.

This pot was made by Maya craft workers, but it shows how Maya potters were affected by other styles of pottery. The patterns are Maya, but putting the pot on three legs is a style copied from the people of Teotihuacán.

Craft workers in different cities had different styles. Also, people who were taken over by the Maya often had their own styles of pottery and weaving. One of the ways to find out where traders from a **city-state** traveled is to see where their local style of pottery is found. Also, craft workers sometimes mixed styles of pots or jewelry. For example, they could use a Maya shape for a pot but decorate it in a style used in places their traders visited.

23

Families and Clothing

The Maya lived and worked in large family groups. This was true of villagers as well as royal and **noble** families. Villages were made up of several of these family groups. This meant that there were enough people to make and grow all the food, cloth, pots, and other goods that everyone needed. The men farmed and made pots while the women cooked and wove cloth and baskets. Children learned from their parents and started to work as soon as they were old enough. Only **scribes** went to school.

This model shows a Maya woman weaving cloth on a "backstrap" loom. She keeps the long threads tight by tying them to her back and to the branch across her feet.

*This pottery model shows an **ajaw** sitting on his throne. You can tell how important he is because his clothes are so fancy and his ear plugs are so big. They were probably made from jade and would have been very heavy.*

Most Maya cloth was made from cotton dyed with vegetable dyes. Ordinary workers wore simple clothes that were easy to work in. Men wore **loincloths,** and women wore long skirts and **tunics.** The more important people wore more layers of clothing, and the cloth was more brightly colored and decorated. **Nobles** wore long skirts and tunics or capes. Both men and women wore jewelry and sandals. Some Maya also wore fancy headdresses. The more complicated the headdress, the more powerful the person wearing it was.

Homes

Most Maya lived in villages in one-roomed rectangular huts. These huts had one door and no windows. The walls were made with branches and clay, and the roof was **thatched** and very steep so that the rain would quickly run off it. The floor was made of dirt and there was a **hearth** for a fire.

Homes of kings, **nobles,** and priests in the city were made from stone. The rooms were the same shape as a village home, but there were more of them. They were usually plastered and painted in bright colors.

Many of the descendants of the ancient Maya still live in huts with thatched roofs, much like their ancestors.

Maya

Most Maya villages were arranged like this one.

Crops were grown around the edges of the village.

Women worked together in the central courtyard.

Homes were small, dark and airless.

The men farmed, while the women ran the homes.

27

Writing and Calendars

The Maya used a form of picture writing called glyphs. It took a long time to translate them, and even today not everyone agrees about what they mean.

The Maya used glyphs everywhere. They are carved on decorated standing stones called stelae, on altars, and on buildings. They are painted around the edges of plates and cups. They are also painted on long, folding books called codices. The Spanish who invaded in 1519 destroyed all but three of these codices.

This carving shows the problems of translating glyphs. No one knew if they should be read from left to right or even if they should be read across or up and down.

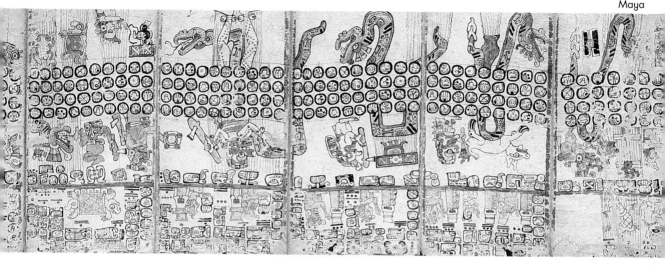

This page from the Madrid Codex has calendar dates running across the middle of the folded page.

The Maya had a very complicated calendar system, with three sets of calendars running at once. There was a "sacred calendar," which had 260 days arranged in 20 months of 13 days. Each day was named after the month and the day. For example, the first day of *Imix,* the first month, was 1 *Imix.* The second day was 2 *Imix,* and so on, up to 13 *Imix.* Then the next month began.

The second calendar was the "vague year." It had 365 days arranged in 18 months of 20 days each, with five extra days at the end of the year. Finally, the Maya had the "long count," which lasted about 400 years. It used differently named and numbered counts of 360 days each.

End of Empire

People lived at Chichén Itzá long after 900 C.E. However, they were influenced by non-Maya people like the Toltecs. This carving is in the Toltec style.

The Maya empire did not end suddenly with a takeover by another group. Instead, it finished as it began, slowly and over many years. By 900 C.E. most cities were abandoned. Some were still lived in but probably ruled by others.

Why did the Maya leave their cities? No one knows for sure. The population grew, and there was not enough food. Studying skeletons has shown that 90 percent of people were underfed. This may have led the villagers to rise up against their kings, who were supposed to control the crops. Wars between the **city-states** could have gotten out of control. But we may never know what caused the end of the Maya.

Glossary

ajaw   Mayan name for their ruler

ceremony   set of acts that has religious meaning

city-state   a city and the towns, villages, and land around it that are controlled by the ruler of the city

famine   time when there is not enough food, so many people go hungry and some die

festival   time of celebration with special events and entertainment

hearth   area in front of a fireplace

irrigate   to bring water to crops

loincloth   short skirt that covers the part of the body between the waist and thighs

noble   important person of high birth or rank

plaza   large open square in the center of a city or town

quilted   made of several layers of cloth stitched together

scribe   person whose job is to read, write, and keep records

shrine   special place for worshipping gods or dead relatives

spirit   being that has life but cannot be seen

temple   building that is the home of gods and goddesses, where people pray to them

terrace   area of flat land made on a hillside so that it can be farmed

thatched   having a roof made out of grass or other plants

tunic   garment shaped like a knee-length T-shirt

volcanic   made from lava

More Books to Read

Ancona, George. *Mayeros: A Yucatec Maya Family.* New York: Lothrop, Lee & Shepard Books, 1997.

An older reader can help you with these books:

Levchuck, Caroline M. *Kids in the Time of the Maya.* New York: Rosen Publishing Group, 1999.

Schuman, Michael A. *Mayan & Aztec Mythology.* Berkeley Heights, N.J.: Enslow Publishers, Inc., 2001.

Index

ajaws   6, 7, 8, 9, 18

ball game   14, 15, 18

calendars   5, 29
ceremonies   6, 7
cities   5, 6, 7, 9, 10, 14, 16, 22, 23, 26
city-states   5, 8, 12, 18, 19, 23, 30
clothes   25

families   24
farming   5, 20, 21, 22
festivals   7, 14, 18
food   9, 21, 22

gods and goddesses   6, 11, 12, 16, 17

houses   11, 16, 17, 26

kings   5, 8, 12, 14, 17, 22, 26

nobles   7, 9, 18, 22, 24, 25, 26

priests   7, 9, 12, 22, 26

schools   24
scribes   24
shrines   13, 16
spirits   13

temples   5, 10, 11, 14, 16, 17
terraces   20
trade   8, 22, 23

villages   9, 14, 20, 22, 24, 26, 27

war   18, 19, 30
writing   5, 28